Hitler's

Munich

Cover Photo

Hitler in the banqueting hall in the Hofbräuhaus in 1936. In 1920 he launched the Nazi party in the same hall on the second floor of this building. See page 40

Published 2007 by Foxley Books

Foxley Books Limited
212 Piccadilly
London W1J 9HG
United Kingdom

www.FoxleyBooks.com

ISBN (10) 1-905742-00-2
ISBN (13) 978-1-905742-00-4

Printed and bound by Lightning Source

'Those who cannot remember the past are condemned to repeat it.'

George Santayana

About the author

Joachim von Halasz was born in 1971 and brought up in Frankfurt/Main. In 1997 he left Germany for London. He worked in Financial PR in the City of London for nine years and now runs his own PR firm. He is married with three children.

In Munich on business trips he discovered the historical sites of the Third Reich hidden from the public eye. Encouraged by friends he began writing this book in 2006.

Foxley Books

Foxley Books is an independent publishing house run by Joachim von Halasz. It is based in London and specialises in travel guide books.

The name Foxley derives from Operation Foxley, the British plan to kill Hitler. In 1944 British intelligence services planned to parachute two snipers near Hitler's mountain retreat at Berchtesgaden to assassinate him.

www.FoxleyBooks.com

Discover more books on www.FoxleyBooks.com.

Contents

Introduction

Today many historical sites in Munich related to the events of the Third Reich have been razed or masked to destroy the memory of where related events took place. The story of the Third Reich has become a history of books, films and pictures. As such it has become disconnected from its geographical place. This disconnection of history from its origins is dangerous. History becomes unreal and questionable. We must maintain the physical contact with the past if we want to avoid repeating it.

This book tells the story and gives the setting of Hitler's time in Munich. It is a period in history that dramatically influenced the events of the 20th century and perhaps still today.

In order to protect our democracy and liberties we should preserve the memory of these historical sites and use them to educate future generations. Everybody has the right to know where these events happened and a moral duty to remember them.

Joachim von Halasz

London, October 16, 2007

Chronology

1889	April 20, Hitler born in Braunau, Austria
1913	**May 25, Hitler arrives in Munich, site 1**
1914	January 18, Hitler unfit for Austrian army in Salzburg
	August 2, Hitler welcomes the Great War, site 3
	August 16, Hitler joins German army, site 5
	October 8, Hitler leaves for the Western Front
1918	October 14, Hitler blinded by mustard gas
	November 21, Hitler returns to Munich, site 7
1919	January 5, Foundation of DAP (German Workers Party), site 9
	September 12, Hitler discovers DAP, site 10
	October, First party headquarters, site 10
	October 16, Hitler's first speech, site 11
1920	Launch of weekly party newspaper, site 12
	Foundation of SA (Storm Troop), site 10
	February 24, Launch of the NSDAP (Nazi Party), site 13
	March 31, Hitler moves to Thiersch Strasse, site 14
1921	February 3, Hitler gives speech to 6,000, site 16
	The party has 4,300 party members
1922	May 22, Foundation of Hitler Youth, site 17
	The party has 18,200 party members
1923	January 28, First Nazi Party rally, site 18
	March, Foundation of SS (Security Squad), site 19
	The party has 55,000 party members
	November 8, Beginning of Beer Hall Putsch, site 17
	November 9, Beer Hall Putsch crushed, site 3
	November 11, Hitler arrested by police outside Munich
1924	February 26, Hitler's trial begins, site 21
	April 1, Hitler sentenced to five years in prison, site 21
	December 19, Hitler released from prison in Landsberg

1925	February 27, Relaunch of Nazi Party, site 17
	July 19, *Mein Kampf* published, site 12
1929	Himmler becomes head of SS (Security Squad), site 23
	Hitler moves to Prinzregenten Platz, site 24
	Hitler meets Eva Braun, site 23
1930	September 14, Nazi Party comes second in General Elections
1931	Fourth party headquarters, Braune Haus, site 30
	Foundation of SD (Security Service), site 32
	September 19, Geli Raubal commits suicide, site 24
1932	July 31, Nazi Party becomes strongest party in Germany
1933	January 30, Hitler becomes Chancellor, Berlin
	Foundation of Gestapo, site 33
1934	June 30, 'Night of the Long Knives', site 30
1935	November 8-9, Inauguration of Temples of Honour, site 34
1937	July 18, Opening of Haus der Deutschen Kunst, site 35
	July, 'Degenerate Art' exhibition, site 36
	Opening of the Führerbau, site 37
	Opening of Hitler's night club, site 40
1938	September 30, Munich Agreement, site 37
	November 9, 'Night of Broken Glass', site 41
1939	September 3, Unity Mitford commits suicide, site 42
	November 8, Elser's bomb explodes, site 17
1943	February 18, Sophie Scholl arrested, site 43
1944	**April 17, Hitler in Munich for the last time, site 3**
1945	April 30, Hitler commits suicide, Berlin
	April 30, US army captures Munich, site 44

In **bold** are the dates of Hitler's arrival in Munich and when he left for the last time.

The **site number** relates to the map reference (pp.12-13) and the historical site index (pp.14-19).

Walks

A visit to the Third Reich exhibition at the **City Museum (site 45)** is recommended to gain an overview over this period.

Convenient places for a break during the walks are the café in the **Haus der Kunst (site 35)**, the **Osteria Italiana (site 38)** restaurant or the **Hofbräuhaus (site 13)** beer hall.

Key events walk - short (1hr)

- First party HQ, Sterneckerbräu, Tal 38, pp.36, 37, 40, site 10
- Launch of Nazi party, Hofbräuhaus (break), Am Platzl 9, p.40, site 13
- Feldherrnhalle, Odeons Platz, pp.22, 24, 26, 28, 46, 49, 77, site 3
- Braune Haus, Brienner Strasse, pp.64, 70, 72, site 30
- Temples of Honour, Brienner Strasse, pp.70, 72, site 34
- Führerbau, Arciss Strasse 12, pp.70, 73, 76, site 37

Key events walk - long (2.5hr)

- Thule Society, Hotel Vier Jahreszeiten, Maximilian Strasse 17, p.36, site 8
- First party HQ, Sterneckerbräu, Tal 38, pp.36, 37, 40, site 10
- Launch of Nazi party, Hofbräuhaus (break), Am Platzl 9, p.40, site 13
- Feldherrnhalle, Odeons Platz, pp.22, 24, 26, 28, 46, 49, 77, site 3
- War Ministry, Ludwig Strasse14, p.48, site 20
- Resistance, Universität, p.77, site 43
- Party HQ, Schelling Strasse 50, pp.60, 61, site 23
- Osteria Italiana (break), Schelling Strasse 62, p.73, site 38
- Barracks, Türken Strasse, p.28, site 5
- Führerbau, Arciss Strasse 12, pp.70, 73, 76, site 37
- Temples of Honour, Brienner Strasse, p.70, 72, site 34
- Braune Haus, Brienner Strasse, pp.64, 70, 72, site 30

Hitler's Munich walk (5hr)

- Hitler arrival & departure, Hauptbahnhof, pp.24, 77, site 1
- **Hitler 1913-14, Schleissheimer Strasse 34, p.24, site 2**
- **Hitler 1914, Elisabeth Platz 4, p.28, site 6**
- **Hitler 1918-20, Loth Strasse 29, p.36, site 7**
- Osteria Italiana (break), Schelling Strasse 62, p.73, site 38
- Party HQ, Schelling Strasse 50, pp.60, 61, site 23
- Barracks, Türken Strasse, p.28, site 5
- Führerbau, Arciss Strasse 12, pp.70, 73, 76, site 37
- Temples of Honour, Brienner Strasse, p.72, site 34
- Braune Haus, Brienner Strasse, pp.64, 70, 72, site 30
- War Ministry, Ludwig Strasse 14, p.48, site 20
- Feldherrnhalle, Odeons Platz, pp.22, 24, 26, 28, 47, 49, 77, site 3
- First party HQ, Sterneckerbräu, Tal 38, pp.36, 37, 40, site 10
- Launch of Nazi party, Hofbräuhaus (break), Am Platzl 9, p.40, site 13
- Thule Society, Hotel Vier Jahreszeiten, Maximilian Strasse 17, p.36, site 8
- Haus der Deutschen Kunst (break), Prinzregenten Strasse 1, pp.73, 78, site 35
- **Hitler 1920-29, Thiersch Strasse 41, pp.40, 52, site 14**
- *Mein Kampf*, Thiersch Strasse 11, pp.40, 60, site 12
- Beer Hall Putsch, Bürgerbräukeller, Rosenheimer Strasse 29, pp.41, 48, 60, 77, site 17
- Speech venue, Hofbräukeller (break), Innere Wiener Strasse 19, p.37, site 11
- **Hitler 1929-45, Prinzregenten Platz 16, pp.61, 65, 74, 76, site 24**

In **bold** are the addresses where Hitler lived.

The **site number** relates to the map reference (pp.12-13) and the historical site index (pp.14-19).

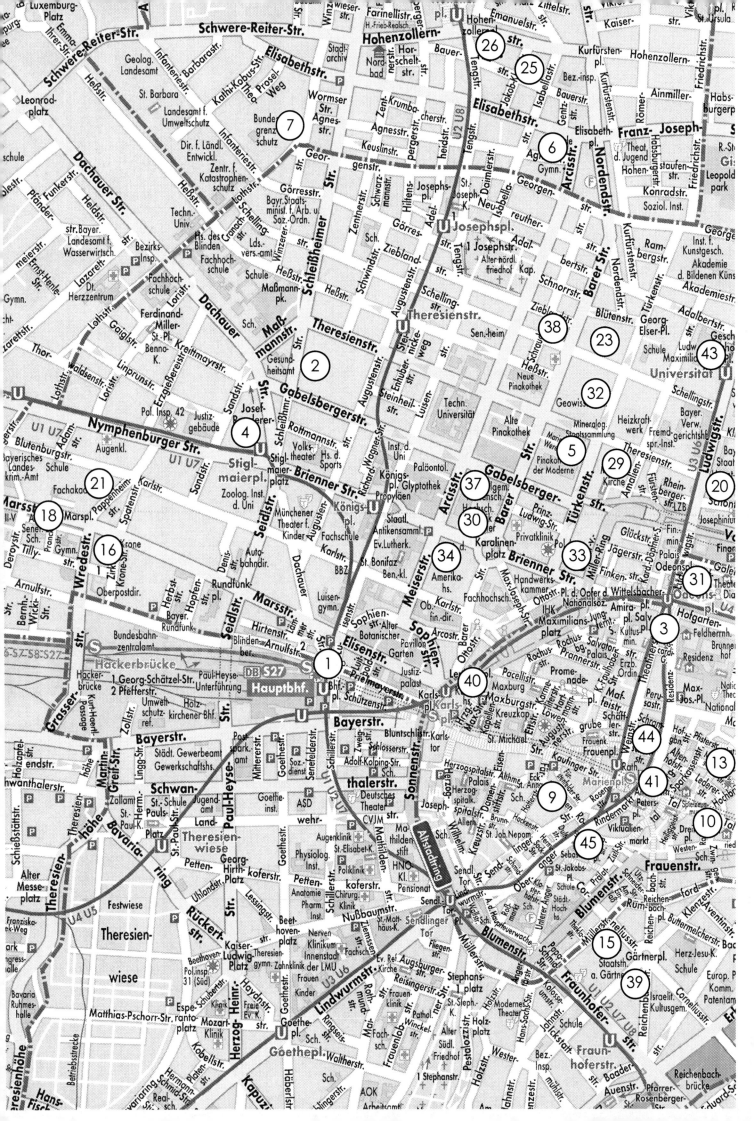

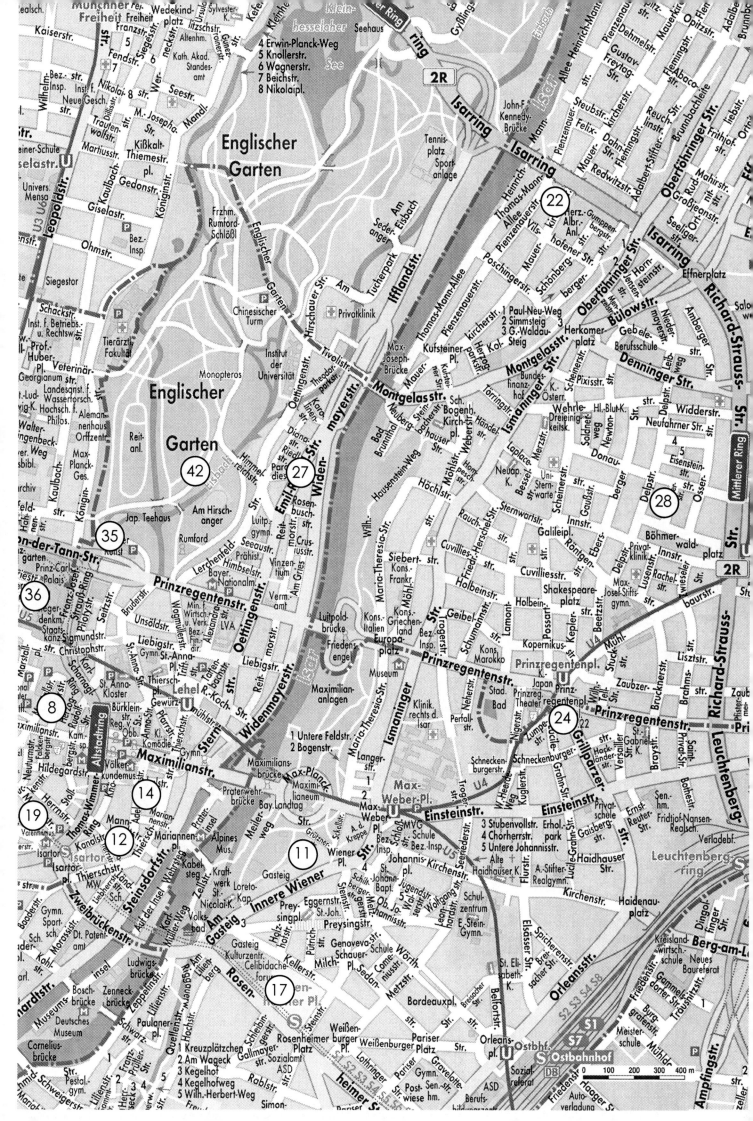

Historical sites

1
Hauptbahnhof
Hitler arrived, 1913, p.24
Hitler left, 1944, p.77

In May 1913 Hitler arrived at the central station for the first time. In April 1944 he left Munich for the last time.

2
Schleissheimer Strasse 34
Hitler, 1913-14, p.24

Hitler's room was on the third floor, second window from the right.

3
Feldherrnhalle
Painting, 1913, pp.22, 24
WW1, 1914, pp.26, 28
Putsch, 1923, pp.46, 48
Funeral, 1944, p.77

The Feldherrnhalle (Hall of Field Marshals) is a key site in Hitler's Munich.

4
Löwenbräukeller
Stiegelmaier Platz
Hitler, 1913, p.25
Putsch, 1923, p.48

This beer hall was one of Hitler's favourites and important during the Beer Hall Putsch.

5
Barracks
Türken Strasse
Hitler, 1914, p.28

Hitler arrived at these barracks to join a Bavarian infantry regiment. It was here that he took his oath to King Ludwig III.

6
School
Elisabeth Platz 4
Hitler, 1914, p.28

During his military training Hitler was based in this school because most barracks were overcrowded.

7
Barracks
Loth Strasse 29
Hitler, 1918-20, p.36

After WW1 Hitler lived in these barracks. It was during this time that he became a politician.

8
Hotel Vier Jahreszeiten
Maximilian Strasse 17
Thule Society, 1919, p.36

In this hotel the Thule Society, earliest supporter of the Nazi Party, met frequently.

9
Fürstenfelder Hof
Fürstenfelder Strasse 14
DAP, 1919, p.36

The Fürstenfelder Hof tavern - where the DAP, the predecessor of the Nazi party, was founded - was replaced with a modern office block.

10
Sterneckerbräu
Tal 38
Hitler,1919, p.36
1st party HQ, 1919, p.37
SA, 1920, p.40

The beer hall were Hitler met the DAP was located on the ground floor of this building.

11
Hofbräukeller
Innere Wiener Strasse 19
Speech, 1920, p.37

Hitler gave his first public party speech in this beer hall.

12
Thiersch Strasse 11
Party weekly, 1920, p.40
Mein Kampf, 1925, p.60

Hitler's book *Mein Kampf* and the Nazi newspaper were published in this house.

13
Hofbräuhaus
Am Platzl 9
Nazi party, 1920, p.40

The Nazi party was launched by Hitler in the banqueting hall on the second floor of this beer hall.

14
Thiersch Strasse 41
Hitler, 1920-29, p.40

Hitler lived in a small room on the first floor, first window from the left, during the early years of the Nazi Party.

15
Cornelius Strasse 12
2nd party HQ, 1920, p.40

The party HQ moved here from Sterneckerbräu (site 10).

16
Zirkus Krone
Mars Strasse 43
Speech, 1921, p.41

This circus hall was the largest venue for Hitler's speeches. Here he could address more than 6,000 people. See picture on page 38.

17
Bürgerbräukeller
Rosenheimer Strasse 29
Hitler Youth, 1922, p.41
Putsch, 1923, p.48
Relaunch, 1925, p.60
Bomb, 1939, p.77

The beer hall was razed in 1979 and a hotel was built on the same site.

18
Mars Platz
Rally, 1923, p.41

The first Nazi Party rally was held on the Mars Platz (see photo page 42). Today the site is covered by roads.

19
Torbräu
Tal 41
SS, 1923, p.41

The SS was founded in the basement of this building.

20
War Ministry
Ludwig Strasse 14
Putsch, 1923, p.48

On the day of the Putsch the War Ministry was occupied by Captain Röhm and Storm Troopers.

21
Pappenheimer Strasse 14
Hitler's trial, 1924, p.49

Hitler went on trial for high treason in this building after the Putsch (see illustration page 50). He received a five-year prison sentence but was released after 12 months.

22
Pienzenauer Strasse 52
Christmas, 1924, p.53

After his release from prison Hitler celebrated Christmas in this villa with the family of his supporter Ernst Hanf-staengl.

23
Schelling Strasse 50
3rd Party HQ, 1925, p.60
Himmler's SS, 1929, p.60
Eva Braun, 1929, p.61

Hitler set up the 3rd Nazi Party HQ in this building and here he met Eva Braun in Hoffmann's photo studio.

24
Prinzregenten Platz 16
Hitler, 1929-45, p.61
Geli Raubal, 1931, p.65
Chamberlain, 1938, p.76

Hitler's nine-room flat on the second floor houses a police station today.

25
Isabella Strasse 45
Eva Braun, 1912, p.61

Eva Braun, Hitler's mistress and wife, was born in this house in 1912.

26
Hohenzollern Strasse 93
Eva Braun, 1925-35, p.61

Eva Braun lived with her parents on the third floor of this building. Here she twice failed to commit suicide.

27
Widenmeyer Strasse 42
Eva Braun, 1935-36, p.61

After Eva Braun's 21st birthday she moved into a flat in this building rented by Hitler. Braun's father tried in vain to persuade Hitler to send her back.

28
Delp Strasse 12
Love nest, 1936-45, p.64

Hitler bought this villa for Eva Braun. It became their love nest.

29
Amalien Strasse 25
Hoffmann, 1930, p.64

Heinrich Hoffmann, Hitler's personal photographer, had his photo shop and studio in this building.

30
Braunes Haus
Brienner Strasse
4th party HQ,1931, p.64

The Reich leadership of the Nazi Party was based in the Braune Haus (see photo page 70). The building was razed to the ground after the war.

31
Odeons Platz 6
Café Heck, 1932, p.65

Hitler held many important and informal meetings with his closest advisors in Café Heck which was based in this building.

32
Türken Strasse 23
SD, 1931, p.65

Reinhard Heydrich, recruited by Himmler to set up the party's internal security service (SD), ran his first office from this building.

33
Brienner Strasse 20
Gestapo, 1933, p.72

Himmler and Heydrich set up the Gestapo in the Wittelsbacher Palais, which stood on this site.

34
Brienner Strasse
Temples,1935, p.72

Two Temples of Honour were built to remember the dead of the Putsch of 1923 (see photo page 70). Both structures were razed to the foundations.

35
Haus der Kunst
Prinzregenten Strasse 1
Nazi art, 1931, p.73

Previously called the Haus der Deutschen Kunst (House of German Art) exhibited artists chosen by Hitler.

36
Galerie Strasse 4
"Degenerate Art", 1937, p.73

A "Degenerate Art" exhibition was staged in these buildings.
Expressionism, impressionism, surrealism and cubism were all considered degenerate.

37
Führerbau
Arciss Strasse 12
Opening, 1935, p.73
Agreement, 1938, p.76

The Munich Agreement was singed in this building.

38
Osteria Italiana
Schelling Strasse 62
Lunch, 1930s, p.73

Hitler's favourite lunch place in the 1930s was the Osteria Bavaria serving Austrian food.

39
Theater am Gärtner Platz
Merry Widow, 1938, p.76

Hitler's favourite musical comedy the 'Merry Widow' was put on stage here.

40
Künstlerhaus
Lenbach Platz 8
Night club, 1938, p.76

Hitler ran his night club in the Künstlerhaus (House of Artists).

41
Altes Rathaus
Marien Platz 15
Crystal Night, 1938, p.76

Goebbels unleashed the purge of Jews in the Festsaal (banqueting hall) of the Old Town Hall.

42
Englische Garten
Unity Mitford, 1939, p.77

Unity Mitford, daughter of English aristocrat Lord Redesdale and close friend of Hitler, shot herself in the head in the Englische Garten.

43
Universität
Scholl, 1943, p.77

Sophie Scholl and her brother were caught while distributing anti-Nazi leaflets in the University building.

44
Neues Rathaus
Marien Platz
Defeat, 1945, p.77

The 7th US army had their headquarters in the New Town Hall from May 1945.

45
Stadtmuseum
Sankt Josef Platz 1
Exhibition

This city museum houses a permanent exhibition: 'Nationalsozialismus in München'.
Open Tuesday to Sunday, 10am to 6pm.

'One does not know German art if one has not seen Munich!'

Hitler, on arrival in Munich, 1913

'He began his painting straight away and stuck to his work for hours.'

Frau Popp, Hitler's landlady, in 1913.
Hitler's watercolour of the Feldherrnhalle
and Theatinerkirche

Adolf Hitler arrived in Munich's **Hauptbahnhof (site 1)** (central station) by train from Vienna on May 25, 1913, together with his friend Robert Häusler. Almost 33 years later, on April 17, 1944, he left Munich for the last time, after the funeral of the Munich Gauleiter Adolf Wagner - this time in his own train (p.77). Since then the station has received a new façade.

During his time in Vienna, Hitler had twice failed to enter the Academy of Arts, instead living in a men's hostel and making a living from painting and selling watercolours. At the age of 24, he decided to move to Munich to evade military service in the Austrian army, which he disliked for its multi-national character. He also considered Vienna to be a melting pot of nationalities and blurred identities held together under the steadily weakening influence of the imperial flag. Munich was the most important artistic city in Europe next to Paris, here he hoped to make his breakthrough as an artist and architect.

North of central station, in Schwabing, the bohemian student district, Hitler and Häusler shared a room in **Schleissheimer Strasse 32 (site 2)**. This was Hitler's first address in Munich. On the registration form he noted as his profession 'architectural painter from Vienna'. A plaque was fixed on the house from 1936 to 1945 mentioning that Hitler had lived here.
Frau Popp, his landlady, remembered:
'The next morning my Herr Hitler went out and came back again in no time with an easel he had picked up somewhere. He began his painting straight away and stuck to his work for hours. In a couple of days I saw two lovely pictures finished and lying on the table, one of the Cathedral and the other of the Theatinerkirche.' (See picture page 22.)

Hitler painted watercolours of most tourists sites including the **Feldherrnhalle** at **Odeons Platz (site 3)**. (See p.22.) The Feldherrhalle (Hall of Field Marshals) is one of the key sites in Hitler's Munich. (See pp. 26, 28, 46, 48, 77.)

Days of painting were followed by days studying books about Marxism in his room:
'I immersed myself in the theoretical literature of this new world. Now for the first time I turned my attention to the attempts to master this world plague.'

In Vienna Hitler had begun to form his ideas about anti-Semitism, nationalism and racism. His Munich landlady observed:
'He just camped in his room like a hermit with his nose stuck in those thick, heavy books and worked and studied from morning to night.'

Hitler would then go to a beer hall or café to engage anyone around in political debates. Thereby he sharpened his ideas and theories. At the time he was a regular in the **Löwenbräukeller** beer hall at **Stieglmaier Platz (site 4).** This beer hall was a key site during the Beer Hall Putsch. (See p.48.)

Once his landlady asked him what all the reading had to do with painting. Hitler replied:
'Dear Frau Popp, does anyone know what is and what isn't likely to be of use to him in life?'

On January 18, 1914, the Munich criminal police arrived at Hitler's door and asked him to present himself for military service in Austria, which was compulsory. If he failed to comply he would be liable to prosecution and a fine for evading military service. A couple of days later Hitler travelled to Salzburg. After a medical test he was found unfit for combat duties and unable to bear arms. Relieved, he returned to Munich.

While Hitler was in Salzburg, Häusler moved out of their shared room, unable to cope any longer with Hitler's habit of staying awake and delivering endless political monologues during the night.

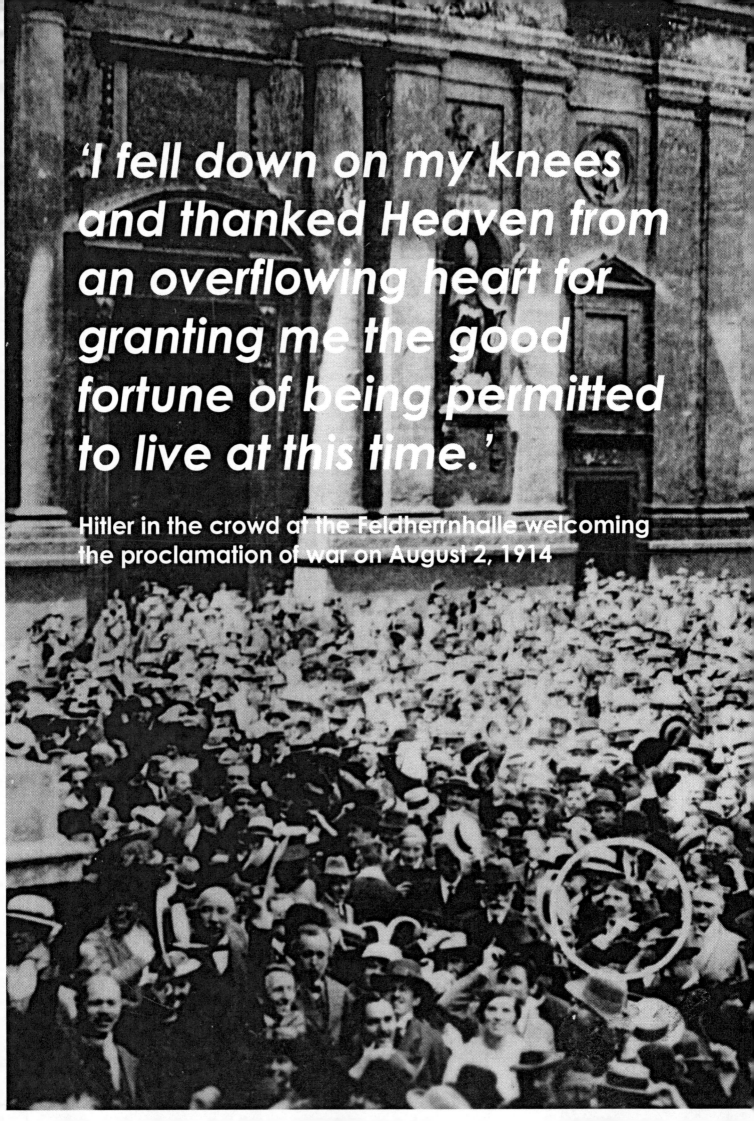

'I fell down on my knees and thanked Heaven from an overflowing heart for granting me the good fortune of being permitted to live at this time.'

Hitler in the crowd at the Feldherrnhalle welcoming the proclamation of war on August 2, 1914

On June 28, 1914, the Austrian duke Franz Ferdinand was assassinated by a Serb terrorist. Austria declared war against Serbia, which prompted a mobilisation of Russia against Austria and Germany against Russia.

On August 2, 1914 news of war with Russia was received with enthusiasm by Hitler as he stood in a large crowd in front of the **Feldherrnhalle** at **Odeons Platz (site 3)** (see photo page 26). He had found a new purpose in his life:
'I fell down on my knees and thanked Heaven from an overflowing heart for granting me the good fortune of being permitted to live at this time.'

The following day war against France was declared and Hitler submitted a personal petition to the Bavarian King Ludwig III, requesting permission to enlist in his army. The following day he was accepted as a volunteer.

Hitler reported to the **barracks** of the Bavarian King's Own Regiment in **Türken Strasse (site 5)** on August 16, 1914. From here he was transferred between several infantry regiments before finally staying with the 16th Bavarian Infantry Regiment. Of the barracks only the main entrance remains.

During his military training he was based in a **school** on **Elisabeth Platz 4 (site 6)**, from August 16 to October 10, 1914, because most barracks were overcrowded. He went through an intensive course of drilling, route marching and bayonet practice. Today a trade school is based in the building.

On October 8, 1914 Hitler took his oath to King Ludwig III, in the **barracks** in **Türken Strasse (site 5)**, and two days later he left for Ypres. Shortly before he arrived in the trenches he wrote a postcard to Frau Popp:
'I'm terribly happy. I hope we get to England.'

At Ypres Hitler became a regimental dispatch carrier, or so-called runner. The telephone lines to battalion and company command posts were often disabled by artillery, and only runners could deliver messages. Hitler escaped death many times. On November 3, 1914 he was promoted to the rank of corporal.

Hitler was wounded for the first time on October 7, 1916. An exploding shell hit him in the thigh. He recovered from his injury in a Berlin hospital before returning to the front line. On August 4, 1918, he received the Iron Cross First Class for bravery shown in delivering an important dispatch through heavy fire.

Blinded by mustard gas on October 14, 1918, he recovered in Pasewalk hospital near Berlin. Later he claimed that during this time he had a vision telling him to go into politics, to liberate the German people and to make Germany great again.

After the war Munich became a republic, King Ludwig III having been forced to abdicate. In Berlin Friedrich Ebert, a socialist, became the first President of the German Republic. Imperial Germany had disappeared overnight.

Hitler returned to Munich on November 21, 1918.

'I'm terribly happy. I hope we get to England.'

Hitler as a soldier (far left) and Fuchsl, his dog

'It was the most decisive resolve of my life. From here there was and could be no turning back.'

Hitler, on joining the DAP (predecessor to the Nazi Party) in 1919

Hitler's DAP
membership card

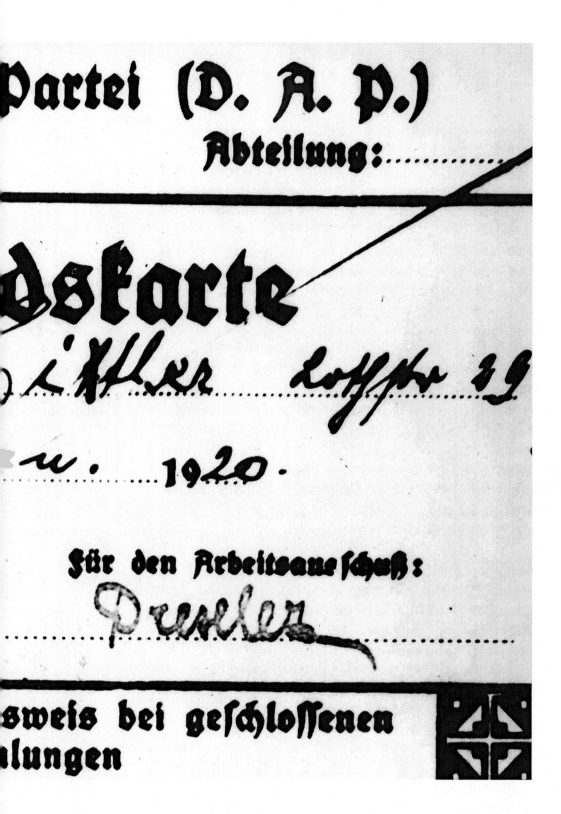

The card is dated January 1, 1920 and signed by Drexler, the founder of the DAP, the predecessor of the Nazi party. In fact Hitler was party member 55 not 555. Still a soldier, his address is given as Loth Strasse 29, the barracks of his regiment.

In 1918 Hitler returned from World War One to Munich and lived in the barracks of his infantry regiment, in **Loth Strasse 29 (site 7)**. In the barracks his roommates again complained about his endless political monologues during the night. Hitler was moved to a single room. It was at this time that he was sent by Captain Karl Mayr to investigate and report on new political parties in Munich. One target was the newly founded DAP (Deutsche Arbeiter Partei / German Workers' Party). Only a part of the barracks has survived and houses offices.

The DAP had been born out of the Thule Society, a secret Munich high-society club that wanted to promote its ideas of a future German master race amongst the working class. This society had been founded the year before by Rudolf von Seboottendorff, and its members met frequently in a suite at the **Hotel Vier Jahreszeiten (site 8)** at **Maximilian Strasse 17**. Today the hotel is still one of Munich's top hotels.

Officially, the DAP was founded by Anton Drexler, a locksmith, and Karl Harrer, a sports journalist, on January 5, 1919, in the **Fürstenfelder Hof (site 9)** tavern at **Fürstenfelder Strasse 14**. Their ideas were nationalistic, anti-Bolshevik and racist. It was little more then a debating club, with no more than 50 members. The original building has been replaced with a modern office block and a post office.

On September 12, 1919 Hitler attended his first DAP party meeting at the **Sterneckerbräu (site 10)** beer hall at **Tal 38**, in a private function room (Leiberzimmer) attached to the main beer hall. During a debate at this meeting he impressed everyone when he argued against the separation of Bavaria from Prussia. He was invited to come to the next meeting, and Drexler gave him a copy of his pamphlet *Mein Politisches Erwachen* (My Political Awakening) which was close to Hitler's ideas. Today a computer shop is based in the premises. (See as well pp. 37, 40)

Shortly thereafter he received a postcard from the DAP, asking him to join the party. Hitler was hesitant:
'Aside from a few directives, there was nothing, no programme, no leaflet, no printed matter at all, no membership cards, not even a miserable rubber stamp, only obvious good faith and good intentions.'

After a second meeting Hitler was still undecided:
'Reason could advise me only to decline, but my feelings left me no rest, and as often as I tried to remember the absurdity of this whole club, my feelings argued for it.'

Soon after Hitler joined the DAP he began turning the debating club into a party machine. A small room was rented in the **Sterneckerbräu (site 10)** beer hall to set up the first party office, including a paid office manager with a typewriter and a telephone.
From now on at least two public party events were organized a month in large beer halls at which Hitler spoke. He decided to advertise these events in newspapers and on posters to attract as many people as possible.

On October 16, 1919 the first large public party event took place, in the **Hofbräukeller (site 11)** beer hall at **Innere Wiener Strasse 19**. In front of more than 100 people Hitler spoke for the first time to a bigger audience. After half an hour he realised:
'...and what before I had simply felt deep down in my heart, without being able to put it to the test, proved to be true; I could speak!'
Hitler's speech left the audience electrified and resulted in generous donations.

'Then you hardly hear more than the breathing of this gigantic multitude, and only when the last word had been spoken did the applause suddenly roar forth.'

Hitler after a speech at Zirkus Krone. The view from his podium, 1921

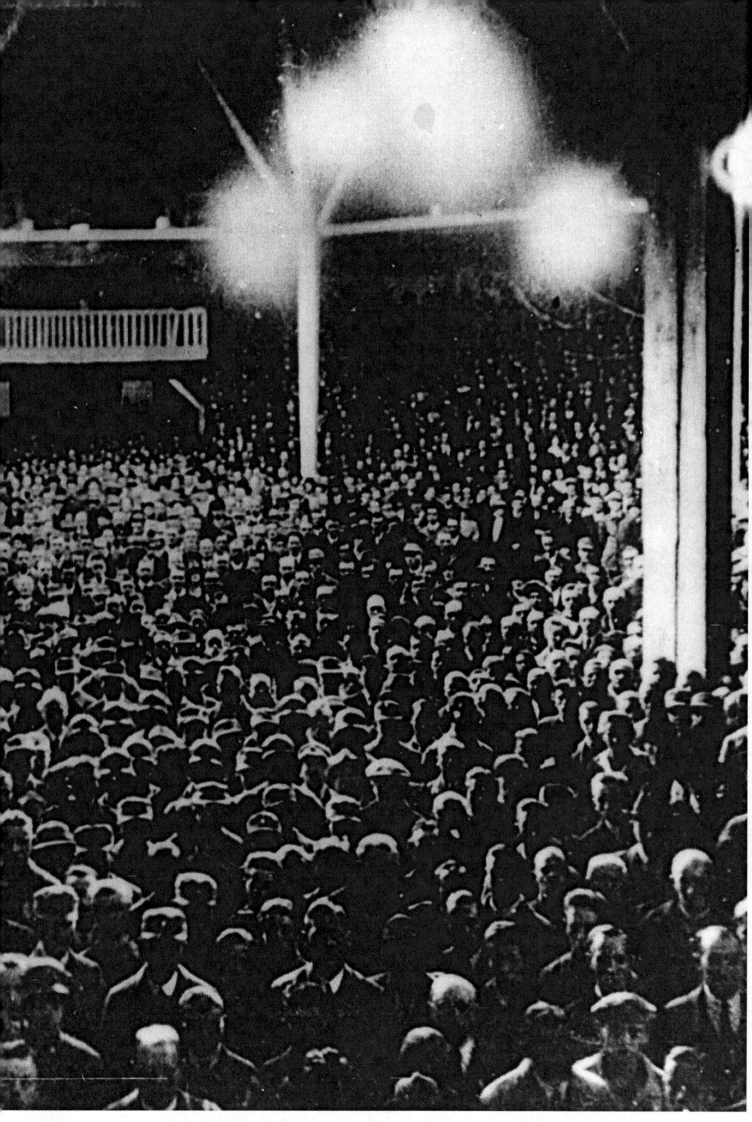

In 1920 the party bought a right wing newspaper, the *Münchener Beobachter* (Munich Observer), from the Thule Society, to spread its political propaganda. They renamed it the *Völkische Beobachter* (People's Observer). A weekly edition was edited in **Thiersch Strasse 11 (site 12)** by Dietrich Eckart, an early supporter of Hitler. Today the same building houses offices and a piano shop. (See as well p. 60.)

The SA (Sturm Abteilung / Storm Troop) was founded by the party in the **Sterneckerbräu (site 10)** beer hall in 1920 to protect Hitler. Storm Troopers silenced hecklers and critics at public meetings.

On February 24, 1920 Hitler launched the 25-point party programme to an audience of 2,000 supporters in the banqueting hall on the second floor of the **Hofbräuhaus (site 13)** beer hall at **Am Platzl 9**. The DAP was renamed NSDAP (National Sozialistische Deutsche Arbeiter Partei / National Socialist German Workers Party; also known as the Nazi Party). Hitler wrote about this evening:
'*A fire was kindled from whose flame one day the sword must come which would regain freedom for the Germanic Siegfried and life for the German people.*'
Today tourists listen to Bavarian folklore music in the same hall every evening.

Shortly thereafter, on March 31, 1920 Hitler was discharged from the army and so he became a full-time politician. He moved out of the barracks and rented a room in **Thiersch Strasse 41 (site 14)**. There Ernst Hanfstaengl, an early supporter, played Wagner operas on the piano to lift Hitler's spirits whenever he was moody. Hitler lived in a small room on the first floor. (See as well p. 53.)

In the same year the party office was moved from Sterneckerbräu to the **Cornelius tavern (site 15)** in **Cornelius Strasse 12**. Here Rudolf Hess, Hermann Göring and Heinrich Himmler joined the party. The original tavern disappeared after WW2.

On February 3, 1921 Hitler spoke for the first time to a mass audience of more than 6,000 people at the **Zirkus Krone (site 16)** at **Mars Strasse 43** (see photo page 38). Two hours later he finished his speech and observed:

'Then you hardly heard more than the breathing of this gigantic multitude, and only when the last word had been spoken did the applause suddenly roar forth to find its release and conclusion in the Deutschland song, sung with the highest fervour.'

Today the circus is known for its clowns and animal shows.

On May 13, 1922 the Nazi Party founded the HJ (Hitler Jugend / Hitler Youth) in the **Bürgerbräukeller (site 17)** beer hall at **Rosenheimer Strasse 29**. Seventeen youngsters joined under the leadership of 18-year-old Gustav Lenk. The beer hall was razed in 1979 and a hotel was built on the same spot. (See as well pp.48, 60, 77.)

The first Nazi Party rally took place January 28, 1923 on the **Mars Platz (site 18)**. More than 20,000 spectators and 5,000 Storm Troopers assembled for the consecration of the flags (see photo page 42). The crowd had to swear that they would never abandon the banners. During the rally, Hitler explained that the colour red stood for the social ideals of the movement, the white represented the nationalist theory and the swastika was a reminder of the struggle for the supremacy of the Aryan man.

In March 1923 the SS (Schutzsatffel / Security Squad), Hitler's personal protection squad, was founded in the **Torbräu (site 19)** beer hall at **Tal 41** by Julius Schreck. They wore black caps with a death's head insignia and they swore unconditional loyalty to Hitler, something not guaranteed by the Storm Troopers under the influence of Captain Ernst Röhm. Today a hotel is operating in the same building.

Party membership increased from 4,300 in 1921 to 18,200 in 1922. By 1923 more than 55,000 members were registered.

The first Nazi party rally

On January 3, 1923, the consecration of the flags took place during the first party rally on the Mars Platz

'Either the German revolution begins tonight or we will all be dead by dawn!'

Hitler, after arresting the Bavarian Government on November 8, 1923

'The national revolution has broken out!'

Hitler during the Beer Hall Putsch

This photomontage tries to capture the moment when the Beer Hall Putsch was crushed by Government troops at the Feldherrnhalle on November 9, 1923. Hitler can be seen wearing a white trench coat

In September 1923 Hitler decided it was time to act against the government in Berlin, to stop the war reparation payments to the Allies that had been imposed on Germany as the defeated nation in World War One. He planned to arrest the leaders of the Bavarian Government and force them to accept him as their leader. Mussolini's march on Rome and formation of a new government in 1922 served as an example for Hitler's attempt to provoke a national revolt and bring down the Berlin Government.

On November 8, 1923 the Bavarian Government held a meeting in the **Bürgerbräukeller (site 17)** beer hall attended by 3,000 officials. Hitler and 600 Storm Troopers surrounded the beer hall and set up a machine gun post at the entrance.

While the Prime Minister of Bavaria gave a speech Hitler, together with Göring, Hess and some Storm Troopers, burst into the hall. Hitler jumped on to a table, fired two shots into the ceiling and shouted:
'The national revolution has broken out! The hall is surrounded.'
The Bavarian government was put under arrest. The so-called Beer Hall Putsch had begun.

Hitler then phoned Captain Röhm, who was with Himmler and another contingent of Storm Troopers at the **Löwenbräukeller (site 4)** beer hall. As agreed Röhm began his march to the **War Ministry (site 20)** at **Ludwig Strasse 14**. On arrival he took control of the ministry, positioned his guards, strung barbed wire around the building and placed machine guns at the windows. Today the building houses the Bavarian State Archives.

On the morning of November 9, 1923 the news reached Hitler that Röhm had taken the War Ministry. Hitler, Göring, Hess and 2,000 men began their march from the **Bürgerbräukeller (site 17)** to support him.

However, Röhm had forgotten to take control of the telephone switchboard in the War Ministry. The officer in charge who had no revolutionary leanings organised a counterattack, summoning loyal army battalions from Augsburg and Regensburg.

When Hitler arrived with his men at the **Feldherrnhalle (site 3)** they were confronted by government troops (see photo page 46). Shots were fired and Hitler was pushed to the ground, dislocating his shoulder. Sixteen Nazis and four policemen died. Today a plaque in the ground remembers the policemen.

During the shooting Hitler escaped by car to a safe house in Uffing. There Helene, the wife of his supporter Hanfstaengel, convinced him not to kill himself with his revolver but to surrender to the police instead. She believed that there was still hope for the Nazi movement. Two days later the police arrested Hitler in Uffing and took him to Landsberg prison.

The Nazi Party, SA, SS and HJ, and the weekly party newspaper, were all outlawed and closed down. At the time almost everyone in Germany believed that this was the end of Hitler and the Nazi movement.

On February 26, 1924 Hitler was put on trial in an infantry school on **Pappenheimer Strasse 14 (site 21)** (see illustration page 50). He was accused of high treason. Hitler found himself in the national spotlight for the first time. Many German newspapers reported on the trial in great detail. Today the building houses offices and a kindergarten.

Georg Neithardt, the presiding judge, allowed Hitler to turn the courtroom into a forum for his personal views and propaganda. Assuming all responsibility, Hitler described to the court what had motivated him. He considered the Bavarian and the Berlin government to have been corrupted by socialist doctrine and declared that he intended to lead Germany back to a position of glory in the world.

Hitler at his trial in 1924

Court artist sketch of Hitler defending himself. He was accused of high treason after the failed Beer Hall Putsch

The judge refused to deport Hitler to Austria and stated:

'Hitler is German-Austrian. In the opinion of the court a man who thinks and feels as German as Hitler, a man who voluntarily served four and a half years in the German army during the war, who earned high war decorations for bravery in the face of the enemy, should not be subjected to the Republic Protection Law.'

On April 1, 1924 Hitler was found guilty of high treason but was sentenced to only five years in Landsberg prison (see photo page 54) instead of receiving the usual death penalty.

In prison he was joined by Hess, who had surrendered to the police after the Putsch. It was during this time that he became Hitler's personal secretary.

During his time in prison Hitler gained influence over his jailers. He converted a majority of the staff to National Socialism and was allowed to leave his lights on until midnight.

He received many female visitors who brought him cakes and sweets. Hitler gained weight and was advised to do some exercise. He refused, insisting that he would soon lose weight when he started giving speeches again.

Throughout the summer of 1924, Hitler prepared himself for the relaunch of the party. He concentrated his efforts on dictating the first part of *Mein Kampf* to Hess on a typewriter. Writing down his political theories was itself a process of self-education.

Hitler was hoping for an early parole for good behaviour. On December 19, 1924 Hitler was released after little more then a year. He was picked up by Heinrich Hoffmann, his photographer, and returned to Munich by car. Outside his house in **Thiersch Strasse 41 (site 14)** he was welcomed by supporters and his room was filled with flowers, cake and wine.

Hitler celebrated Christmas with Hanfstaengl's family in **Pienzenauer Strasse 52 (site 22)**. Alone with Hanfstaengl's wife Helene, he dropped to his knees and put his head in her lap saying:

'If I only had someone to take care of me.'

To her question why he didn't marry, he responded:

'I can never marry because my life is dedicated to my country.'

Hitler's cell in Landsberg prison from 1924

'It's no use sitting still, doing nothing; I want power and I am determined to get it.'

Hitler to Hoffmann in Café Heck, 1932

Hitler rehearsing a speech in 1927

After his release from prison Hitler changed his mind about how to gain power in Germany. He was now convinced that in order to rule Germany he must do everything legally in order to gain credibility and respectability. He wanted to turn the Nazi Party into a seemingly respectable and electable movement, declining to use armed revolution again.

When Hitler was released from prison he immediately set up a centralised infrastructure for the party. Instead of having a party office in the back of a beer hall, he rented 12 rooms in the building in **Schelling Strasse 50 (site 23)** in which his personal photographer, Hoffmann, had his studio. The SA, HJ and SS were relaunched and their offices were set up in the same building next to the party membership office. The party began to organise itself all over Germany in 42 regional districts called 'Gaue'. The Reich leadership oversaw all districts from the new offices.

On February 27, 1925 the Nazi Party was officially relaunched in the **Bürgerbräukeller (site 17)**. The beer hall was jammed with more than 4,000 people to hear Hitler give a speech that unified the party and established himself as its unique leader.

On July 19, 1925, the first volume of Hitler's book, *Mein Kampf*, was published by the Eher publishing house based in **Thiersch Strasse 11 (site 12)**. The second volume of *Mein Kampf* was published on December 11, 1926. In 1930 both books appeared in one edition. Sales of the book made Hitler a millionaire.

On May 20, 1928 the Nazi Party received 2.6 per cent of the votes in the Reichstag elections, winning 12 seats.

Himmler became head of the SS in 1929 with offices in **Schelling Strasse 50 (site 23)**. Under him, the membership of the SS increased from around 200 to 52,000 in 1932 and to 209,000 in 1933. He ordered the construction of Dachau concentration camp outside Munich in 1933. (See page 89 for Dachau tour details.)

In 1929 Hitler moved from Thiersch Strasse into a nine-room flat on **Prinzregenten Platz 16 (site 24)**. (See as well pp.65, 76.) The SS guard that accompanied Hitler had its quarters on the ground floor. In the basement were kitchens and beneath these were air raid shelters. When Lee Miller, a US war correspondent, arrived in Hitler's flat in May 1945 she observed:

'Superficially, almost anyone with a medium income could have been the proprietor of this flat. It lacked grace and charm, it lacked intimacy and was not grand'

Today a police station is based there,

In October of that year Hitler first met Eva Braun, his future mistress, in Hoffmann's office in **Schelling Strasse 50 (site 23)** (see photo page 62). Braun was 17 and was working as an assistant to Hoffmann. Hitler, then 41 years old, immediately took an interest in her. At their first meeting Braun, ignorant of politics, failed to recognise Hitler. He wooed her with flowers and invited her for lunches - the beginning of 15-year affair that would end with a one-day marriage and joint suicide.

Braun was born into a middle class family on February 7, 1912, in **Isabella Strasse 45 (site 25)**. Her father was a school teacher and Braun was the second of three daughters.

From 1925 to 1935 Braun lived with her parents and two sisters on the third floor in **Hohenzollern Strasse 93 (site 26)**. After beginning an affair with Hitler in 1930 she twice attempted to commit suicide - in 1933 with a pistol and 1935 with sleeping pills - feeling abandoned by him.

In 1935, following the second attempt, Hitler rented her a three-bedroom flat in **Widenmeyer Strasse 42 (site 27)** in order to see her more often. Braun was 21 years old and her parents begged her not go.

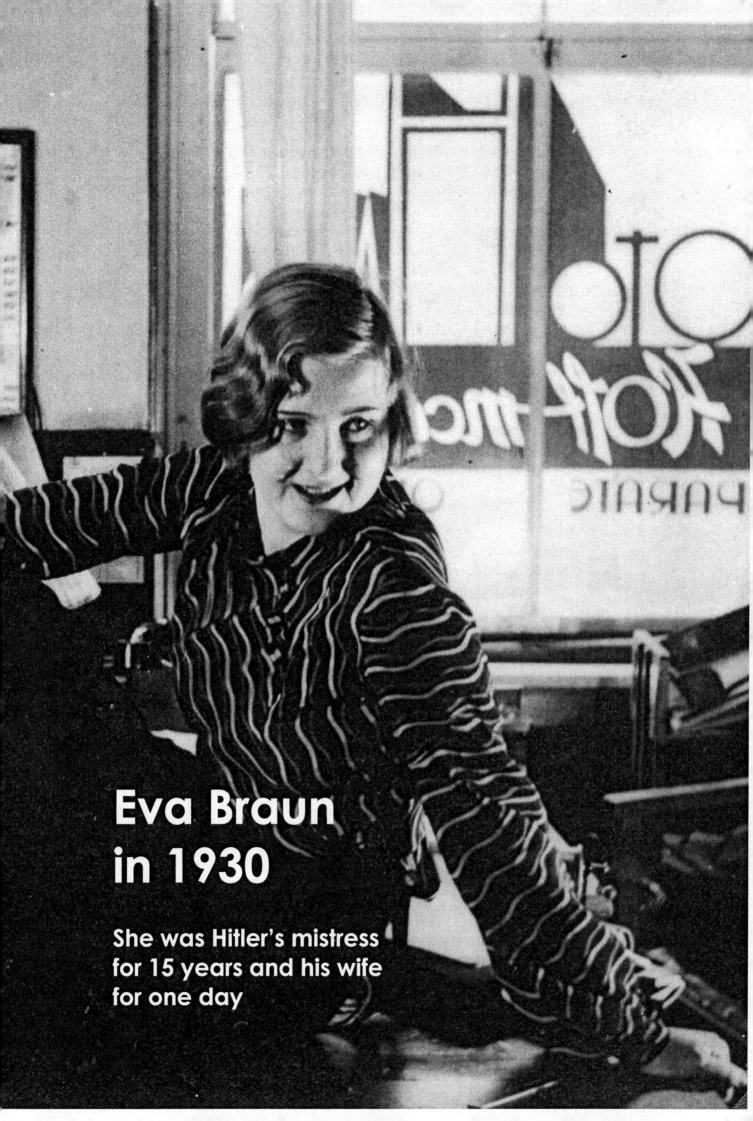

Eva Braun
in 1930

She was Hitler's mistress
for 15 years and his wife
for one day

On March 30, 1936 Braun moved into a villa in **Delp Strasse 12 (site 28)**. Bought for her by Hitler, this place became their love nest. In May 1945, Lee Miller, US war correspondent, visited the house:

'The rooms were small, unspacious and as well furnished as a newly bought suburban house. The furniture and decoration were strictly department store, like everything in the Nazi regime.'

After the war the Bavarian Government confiscated the property.

In 1929 Hoffmann, Hitler's personal photographer, moved his photo studio and shop to **Amalien Strasse 25 (site 29)**. From 1933 he was put exclusive in charge of all press photos for the Nazi Party. He opened studios in Berlin, Paris and Vienna to project the Nazi movement visually. In total he took 2.5 million photos of Hitler and the Nazi movement.

In the election of September 14, 1930 the party received 18.3 per cent of the votes and became the second most powerful party, with 107 seats in the German Reichstag.

A year later the Reich leadership of the Nazi Party moved from Schelling Strasse (site 23) into the **Braune Haus** in **Brienner Strasse (site 30)** (see photo page 71), previously called Barlow Palais. The Nazis bought the three-floor building with the financial help of German industrialists. Paul Troost, Hitler's favourite architect, was in charge of the interior design. The Braune Haus contained several offices, a large Hall of Honour and a senate room with 60 chairs in red leather around a vast conference table. Hitler's office was decorated with portraits of Frederick the Great. He rarely arrived before 11am and would keep people waiting for hours on hand.

The building was razed after the war. The steps that let to the house are still visible in front of the hedge.

Hitler's most crucial political discussions with his closest supporters were held in **Café Heck** at **Odeons Platz 6 (site 31)**. In a secluded corner of its long and narrow room Hitler had a reserved table. During the summer he had a table outside, on the terrace in the Hofgarten. Today Schumann's Bar is operating on the same premises.

In 1931 Reinhard Heydrich set up the party's internal security service, the SD (Sicherheitsdienst / Security Service), in **Türken Strasse 23 (site 32)**. The job had been offered to him by Himmler. Heydrich collected information on friend and foe in a cigar-box filing system and, as a result many spies working for the police or communists inside the Nazi Party were unmasked.

On September 19, 1931 Geli Raubal, Hitler's niece, was found dead with a bullet wound close to her heart in her room in Hitler's flat at **Prinzregenten Platz 16 (site 24)**. She had lived with her uncle since 1929 and it was rumoured that she had had an affair with him. It is unclear if she committed suicide or if she was killed.

On July 31, 1932 the Nazi Party, with 37.4 per cent of the vote, became the strongest political force in Germany. On January 30, 1933 Hindenburg, the aging President of Germany appointed Hitler as Chancellor (see photo page 66).

Hitler is made Chancellor by Hindenburg, in Berlin, 1933

'Munich is Hitler's playground.'

Ernest Pope, American journalist, in Munich from 1936 to 1940

Ceremony at the Temples of Honour in 1935

The Braune Haus, Party HQ, can be seen between the temples. On the left the Führerbau

In 1933 Heydrich and Himmler set up the Gestapo (Geheime Staats Polizei / Secret State Police) in the **Wittelsbacher Palais (site 33)** on **Brienner Strasse 20**. This party police force implemented its own punishment system. Many critics of the regime were locked away in the cellars of the building and tortured, such as Georg Elser (page 77), the beer hall bomber, and Sophie Scholl (page 77), the student activist. The palais was replaced with an office block. A memorial plaque records the dark history of the previous building.

A year later the contest between Hitler and Röhm, for leadership of the four-million-strong Storm Troopers, found its climax in 'The Night of the Long Knives'. On June 30, 1934 Röhm was arrested and brought to the **Braune Haus (site 30)** (see photo page 71) where he was accused by Hitler of plotting to kill him. Röhm denied all charges but Hitler decided to have him shot. Röhm was assassinated on the same day in Stadelheim prison in Munich. As result the power of the SA was broken and the SS became an independent organisation.

In 1935 two neoclassical **Ehrentempel (site 34)** (Temples of Honour) on **Brienner Strasse** were built to display the 16 cast-iron sarcophagi holding the bodies of the Putsch 'martyrs'. Designed by Troost, each temple consisted of 24 columns supporting a heavy architrave. The two temples became a centrepiece of Nazi ritual worship the altars of the movement (see photo page 70). At their inauguration, on November 8 and 9, 1935 Hitler and several thousand soldiers marched from the Feldherrnhalle to the temples, a ceremony that would be repeated every year on the same day. Munich became the official capital of the movement. Both structures were dynamited in 1947 but the foundations are still visible.

On July 18, 1937 the **Haus der Deutschen Kunst (site 35)** at **Prinzregenten Strassse 1**, also built by Troost, opened with the first annual German Art Exhibition. All artists were selected by Hitler. The building was nicknamed 'the Greek railway station' and 'the house of German tarts' because of its external appearance and many nudes exhibited inside. In 1933, at the laying of the foundation stone, Hitler declared Munich the capital of German art. The last annual art exhibition was staged here in 1944.

Today it is dedicated to modern art. A café at the back of the building has survived with original wall paintings.

An exhibition of 'Degenerate Art' opened on July 19, 1937 in **Galerie Strasse 4 (site 36)**, during the first German Art Exhibition. On show were 650 paintings and sculptures by 112 artists that were considered out of line with Nazi ideology. Young people under 18 years of age were barred from the exhibition to underline the obscenity of the artists. The exhibition travelled to 12 German cities and attracted two million visitors.

In 1937 two almost identical neoclassical buildings, again by Troost, were opened - the **Führerbau (site 37)** (Leadership Building) (see as well p.76) in **Arciss Strasse 12** and an administration building in Meiser Strasse. Inside the Führerbau, Hitler and every minster had an office to ensure that the government could move from Berlin to Munich at short notice.

Today the Academy of Music occupies the building. Room 105, on the first floor above the entrance, is where the agreement was signed, It is used for piano rehearsals.

During these years the **Osteria Bavaria (site 38)** restaurant in **Schelling Strasse 62** became Hitler's favourite lunching place. He always came with his entourage and sat at the same table. In 1935 Unity Mitford was introduced to Hitler in this restaurant (see page 77). Today the restaurant is called Osteria Italiana.

Hitler and Chamberlain sign a peace deal in Hitler's flat in 1938

From 1937 onwards Hitler repeatedly enjoyed his favourite comic opera, 'The Merry Widow' at the **Theater am Gärtner Platz (site 39)**. A special highlight was Dorothy van Bruck, an erotic dancer, with her striptease number. Sometimes her costume consisted of a pair of transparent butterfly wings, but more often she was in the nude. Hitler watched Dorothy with his binoculars when she performed her famous back-bending number in the spotlight. Today the theatre is still operating and 'The Merry Widow' is still on the programme but without striptease.

Hitler opened a night club in the **Künstlerhaus (site 40)** on **Lenbach Platz 8** in June 1938. Parties were held in an ornate hall decorated in the height of style and comfort and entertainment was provided by the dancers of the Theater am Gärtner Platz. The details of hundreds of Munich girls were kept on file, and the prettiest were invited to attend the parties. The venue developed into a hotbed of intrigue and orgies. Today the rooms can be hired for private functions.

On September 30, 1938 the Munich Agreement was signed by Hitler, Chamberlain, Mussolini and Daladier in the **Führerbau (site 37)**. The agreement forced Czechoslovakia to cede the Sudetenland to Germany. On the same day Chamberlain and Hitler signed another agreement at **Prinzregenten Platz 16 (site 24)**, in Hitler's flat, stating that Britain and Germany must never go to war with one another again (see photo page 74).

On November 9, 1938 Goebbels unleashed the biggest purge of Jews in Germany from the **Altes Rathaus (site 41)** (Old Town Hall) at **Marien Platz** on the day of the annual commemoration of the Beer Hall Putsch. During the so-called Reichskristallnacht (Night of Broken Glass) 267 synagogues were burnt down, 91 Jews were killed and more than 20,000 Jews transported to concentration camps. Today the room can be hired for private functions. A toy museum is based in the tower.

On September 3, 1939 Unity Mitford, a 25-year-old daughter of English aristocrat Lord Redesdale, shot herself in the head with a pistol, on a bench in the **Englische Garten (site 42)**. Her sister Diana was married to Oswald Mosley, the British fascist leader, and Mitford had been a close friend of Hitler since 1935. She secretly wished to marry him, and the declaration of war between England and Germany had been too much for her to bear. Mitford survived the suicide attempt and was discreetly transfered back to London via Switzerland. Today the park is the main recreation area of Munich.

On November 8, 1939 Georg Elser's bomb exploded in the **Bürgerbräukeller (site 17)** beer hall during a Nazi Party meeting. Eight people were killed and 62 injured, but it missed Hitler, who had left earlier. Elser was caught and handed over to the Gestapo. He was killed in Dachau in 1945.

On February 18, 1943 the students Hans and Sophie Scholl distributed 1,800 copies of their sixth leaflet in the **Universität (site 43)** building, denouncing the Nazi regime and calling for resistance. They were caught and handed over to the Gestapo. After a show trial they were beheaded in Stadelheim prison. Since 1977 a permanent exhibition in the university building remembers the siblings and their work.

Hitler visited Munich for the last time on April 17, 1944 to attend the funeral service of Adolf Wagner, Gauleiter of Munich. It was held at the **Feldherrnhalle (site 3)**. Afterwards he left by train from **Hauptbahnhof (site 1)**.

On April 30, 1945 Munich was taken and occupied by the 7th US army, and their military administration moved into the **Neues Rathaus (site 44)** (New Town Hall) at **Marien Platz**. General Dwight Eisenhower wrote on the day of the city's defeat:
'All of the Allied forces congratulate the 7th Army for the capture of Munich, the cradle of the Nazi beast.'

Hitler leaving the Haus der Deutschen Kunst in 1942

Glossary of abbreviations

DAP (Deutsche Arbeiter Partei) - German Workers Party

Gauleiter - Nazi Party regional leader

Gestapo (Geheime Staats Polizei) - Secret State Police

HJ (Hitler Jugend) - Hitler Youth

NSDAP (National Sozialistische Deutsche Arbeiter Partei) - Nazi Party

SA (Sturm Abteilung) - Storm Troop

SD (Sicherheits Dienst) - Security Service

SS (Schutz Staffel) - Security Squad

Address sources

site 1 - Toland, p.52
site 2 - Stadtmuseum Stadtplan, 2
site 3 - Stadtmuseum Stadtplan, 71
site 4 - Toland, p.54
site 5 - Toland, p.58
site 6 - Joachimsthaler, p.110
site 7 - Weyerer 1919-1933, p.159
site 8 - Weyerer 1919-1933, p.105
site 9 - Münchener Adressbuch 1919
site 10 - Weyerer 1919-1933, p.97
site 11 - Weyerer 1919-1933, p.41
site 12 - Weyerer 1919-1933, p.53
site 13 - Weyerer 1919-1933, p.99
site 14 - Weyerer 1919-1933, p.57
site 15 - Weyerer 1919-1933, p.35
site 16 - Weyerer 1919-1933, p.112
site 17 - Weyerer 1919-1933, p.45
site 18 - Weyerer 1919-1933, p.109
site 19 - Höhne, p.20
site 20 - Weyerer 1919-1933, p.132
site 21 - Weyerer 1919-1933, p.115
site 22 - Münchener Adressbuch 1924
site 23 - Weyerer 1919-1933, p.173
site 24 - Weyerer 1919-1933, p.12
site 25 - Gun, p.19
site 26 - Lambert, p.49
site 27 - Lambert, p.144
site 28 - Weyerer 1933-1949, p.287
site 29 - Bayerische Staatsbibliothek, hoff-6727
site 30 - Weyerer 1919-1933, p.142
site 31 - Münchener Adressbuch 1922
site 32 - Stadtmuseum Stadtplan, 7
site 33 - Weyerer 1933-1949, p.107
site 34 - Rosenfeld, p.85
site 35 - Weyerer 1933-1949, p.151
site 36 - Weyerer 1933-1949, p.124
site 37 - Weyerer 1933-1949, p.92
site 38 - Michielis, p.12
site 39 - Pope, p.1
site 40 - Pope, p.6
site 41 - Weyerer 1933-1949, p.49
site 42 - Pryce-Jones, p.233
site 43 - Weyerer 1933-1949, p.137
site 44 - Weyerer 1933-1949, p.47

Image sources

Cover - Hitler - Bayerische Staatsbibliothek München/Fotoarchiv Hoffmann

Map - Mobilitäts Verlag Berlin 2006

Photos of 45 sites - Foxley Archive

Ch1
Watercolour - Bayerische Staatsbibliothek München/Fotoarchiv Hoffmann
Feldherrnhalle - Bayerische Staatsbibliothek München/Fotoarchiv Hoffmann
Hitler - Bayerische Staatsbibliothek München/Fotoarchiv Hoffmann

Ch2
Membership card - Bayerische Staatsbibliothek München/Fotoarchiv Hoffmann
Zirkus Krone - Bayerische Staatsbibliothek München/Fotoarchiv Hoffmann
Rally - Bayerische Staatsbibliothek München/Fotoarchiv Hoffmann

Ch3
Putsch - Bayerische Staatsbibliothek München/Fotoarchiv Hoffmann
Trial - Süddeutsche Zeitung - SVBilderdienst München
Prison - Bayerische Staatsbibliothek München/Fotoarchiv Hoffmann

Ch4
Hitler - Bayerische Staatbibliothek München/Fotoarchiv Hoffmann
Eva Braun - Bayerische Staatsbibliothek München/Fotoarchiv Hoffmann
Hindenburg - Bayerische Staatsbibliothek München/Fotoarchiv Hoffmann

Ch5
Temples - Bayerische Staatsbibliothek München/Fotoarchiv Hoffmann
Chamberlain - Bayerische Staatsbibliothek München/Fotoarchiv Hoffmann
Hitler - Bayerische Staatsbibliothek München/Fotoarchiv Hoffmann

Quote sources

page 21 - Hitler, p.116
page 22, 24 - Toland, p.53
page 25 - Hitler, p.154
page 25 - Toland, p.54
page 25 - Toland, p.55
page 26, 28 - Hitler, p148
page 28, 31 - Toland, p.59
page 33 - Hitler, p.204
page 37 - Hitler, p.201
page 37 - Hitler, p.202
page 37 - Hitler, p.323
page 40 - Hitler, p.336
page 38, 41 - Hitler, p.456
page 45 - Kershaw, Hubris, p.207
page 47, 48 - Toland, p.156
page 52 - Toland, p.193
page 53 - Toland, p.204
page 57 - Hoffmann, p.64
page 61 - Miller, p.191
page 64 - Miller, p.198
page 69 - Pope, p.1
page 77 - www.shoa.de

Bibliography

Adam, Peter, *The Arts of the Third Reich*, London 1992
Baedeker, *Southern Germany*, Leipzig 1929
Burden, Hamilton, *The Nuremberg Party Rallies*, London 1967
Burleigh, Michael, *The Third Reich: A New History*, London 2001
Gun, Neri, *Eva Braun: Hitler's Mistress*, London 1969
Hamann, Brigitte, *Hitlers Wien*, München 1996
Hanfstaengl, Ernst, *Zwischen Weissem und Braunem Haus*, München 1997
Hoffmann, Heinrich, *Hitler Was My Friend*, London 1955
Haymann, Ronald, *Hitler and Geli*, London 1997
Hitler, Adolf, *Mein Kampf*, London 2004
Höhne, Heinz, *The Order of the Death's Head*, London 1969
Joachimsthaler, Anton, *Hitlers Weg begann in München*, München 2000
Kershaw, Ian, *Hitler 1889-1936: Hubris*, London 2001
Kershaw, Ian, *Hitler 1936-1945: Nemesis*, London 2001
Large, David Clay, *Hitlers München*, München 2001
Lambert, Angela, *The Lost Life of Eva Braun*, London 2006
Michielis, Stefano de, *Osteria Italiana*, München 1998
Miller, Lee, *Lee Miller's War*, London 2005
Münchner Adressbuch, edition 1900 to 1937
Nerdinger, Winfried, *Bauen im Nationalsozialismus*, München 1993
Nerdinger, *Ort und Erinnerung*, München 2006
Pope, Ernst, *Munich Playground*, New York 1942
Pryce-Jones, David, *Unity Mitford*, London 1976
Rosenfeld, Gavriel, *Munich and Memory*, Berkley 2000
Toland, John, *Adolf Hitler*, New York 1976
Stadtkarte München, 1908/1909, 1934/1938, 1993, 2006
Stadtmuseum, Stadtplan Nationalsozialismus in München, München 2004
Weyrer, Benedikt, *München 1919-1933*, München 1993
Weyrer, Benedikt, *München 1933-1949*, München 1996

You've read the book, now come on the tour

Hitler and the Third Reich Walking Tour
Dachau Concentration Camp Memorial Site Tour

Discover for yourself the hidden history mapped in this book with the assistance of a professional guide. We are an English language tour company specialising in walking tours themed on Munich's rich and troubled history.

We pioneered the concept of both English language Third Reich walking tours and guided trips to the Dachau Concentration Camp Memorial Site, with which we have a close working relationship.

All major guide books endorse us. Only the best guides work for us.

Hitler and the Third Reich Walking Tour – a two-and-a-half-hour walking tour through the centre of Munich focusing on the birth of the Nazi movement and its rise to power in the city.

Dachau Concentration Camp Memorial Tour – a five-hour tour (including transport on the 18km journey there and back) through all surviving buildings of the former concentration camp, led by a guide trained and authorised by the Memorial Site itself.

We also offer a wide variety of historic and cultural tours on a range of other themes (including Bavarian beer and food, and day trips to Salzburg.).
In addition to fixed scheduled tours, we also specialise in pre-arranged private tours, tailored to the specific needs of individuals or groups. We have a great deal of experience in working with schools and colleges.

For more details regarding our programme, pricing structure, discounts and special offers, please visit our website: **www.radiusmunich.com**

Radius Tours and Bike Rental
Arnulfstrasse 3
Munich Central Train Station (Hauptbahnhof)
By Track 32
80335 München
Tel (Tours): +49 (0) 89-55 02 93 74
Tel (Bike Rental): +49 (0) 89-59 61 13
Fax: +49 (0) 89-59 47 14
Email: tours@radiusmunich.com

Printed in the United Kingdom
by Lightning Source UK Ltd.
124537UK00001B/135-194/A